KNOW
YOUR
WORTH

KNOW
YOUR
WORTH

Whose Report Will You Believe?

SHIRLEY D.

Library of Congress Control Number: 2021925316
ISBN: Hardcover   978-1-6698-0414-7
                 Softcover   978-1-6698-0413-0
                 eBook   978-1-6698-0412-3

Print information available on the last page.

Rev. date: 12/28/2021

To order additional copies of this book, contact:
Xlibris
844-714-8691
www.Xlibris.com
Orders@Xlibris.com
836586

CONTENTS

DEDICATION

This book is dedicated to the one who allows me to move and live and have my being (Acts 17:28, KJV). With all my love and all that the Lord has downloaded in me, I give it back to Jesus in the writing of this book to help his children. I also dedicate this book to my son, Zaire P. Mills, who I pray knows his worth in the Lord. Thank you both for being my champions to impact positive, life-giving change in the lives of others.

INTRODUCTION

In the beginning, God created you and me! God said, "Let us make mankind in our image, in our likeness, so that they may rule over all creatures" (Gen. 1:26, NIV). God was, in the beginning establishing our worth in life. In search of what "our image" meant, I took a road trip through the Bible to see that the Father, the Son, and the Holy Spirit was working on our behalf in the beginning of time.

The Trinity was working things out for our good (Rom. 8:28, KJV), even before the foundation of the world! Psalm 139:13–16 (ESV), declares, "For you formed my inward parts; you knitted me together in my mother's womb. I praise you, for I am fearfully and wonderfully made. Wonderful are your works; my soul knows very well. My frame was not hidden from you, when I was being made in secret, intricately woven in the depths of the earth. Your eyes saw my unformed substance; in your book were written, every one of them, the days that were formed for me, when as yet there was none of them."

In order for us to know our value, we must be spiritually able to accept the work God did on our behalf, predestining our lives and calling us to be greater in him. God our Father took the time to fashion and mold us the way he wanted us to be because at any time he could've made us look exactly the same. He decided to uniquely make each one of us and purposely place us in the families he wanted us to be a part of. You were no accident or mistake, you are purposed and destined in God. How awesome is it to be hand-selected by God our creator himself.

We tend to oversell ourselves and at times undervalue our worth, so to maintain a balance, we need to get our definition of who we are from Jesus who is the truth and incapable of lying. Let's take our value of ourselves from the giver of life and run on in the precepts and guidance of the word of God to maintain a holy standard of living. If we look back at the beginning when God was creating, he said, "It was good," but when he created man, he said, "It is very good."

In this race we are in to receive eternal life, we must stay on course, walking in right standing with Jesus to receive our prize. Jesus gives us the necessary tools to live a victorious life, with no more having to live by the devil's devices. Scripture says in Proverbs 23:7 (NKJV), "as a man thinketh in his heart, so is he . . ." therefore let's gird up our minds with the word of God, that our hearts would hide the word of God in it, that we would not sin against God (Ps. 119:11, NIV).

"Let your gentleness be evident to all. The Lord is near. Do not be anxious about anything, but in every situation, by prayer and petition, with thanksgiving, present your requests to God. And the peace of God, which transcends all understanding, will guard your hearts and minds in Christ Jesus. Finally, brothers and sisters, whatever is true, whatever is noble, whatever is right, whatever is pure, whatever is lovely, whatever is admirable—if anything is excellent or praiseworthy—think about such things" (Phil. 4:5–8, NIV). These passages help us to intentionally set our minds in gear for a victorious walk. Are you able to capture in your mind, who all these attributes point to?

It is Jesus, nobody but Jesus, who determines our value and worth! I pray that people who feel they need to be defined by mankind are especially listening at this time. Depending on people to define you can leave you: broken, beaten, torn, crushed, and dying in vital areas of your life, unless, you know God as your refuge, and very present help in trouble, (Ps.46:1, KJV). Look to Jesus, keep your eyes focused on him through the word of God, and walk in victory, praying all the time, about everything!

Know Your Worth
Whose Report Will You Believe?

In our life, from infancy to adulthood, there will be many characters and things that would seek to shape who we become in life: family, friends, coworkers, jobs, wealth, health, ourselves, and God. You hold the key to who or what you allow to define or place a value on you. I use to laugh at my older sister as she would lift her two daughters up in the mirror daily, and tell them, "You are pretty, and mama loves you." Remembering those mirror times made me think about how we are supposed to affirm our children that they would know how precious they are, even at birth. When we tell those we love, how great they are, they will not have to seek the approval of the world, or need to be validated by anyone in it. In our journey through life, we will develop relationships with people, and some will have their own deceptive plans for our relationship with them, benefitting themselves. We must be mindful of who we give access, to define us, for that definition may stick with us for the rest of our life.

Stay focused and God-conscious as we determine in our mind to be obedient to God's plans for us. Reading, studying, meditating, and applying the word of God daily; by seeking the help of the

Holy Spirit in prayer, asking him for wisdom, knowledge, and understanding of the word of God, will assist us in direction and staying focused on our goals. We are all in a race in life; a race of grace to find our purpose and to reach our God-given destiny. Ephesians 1:11 (NLT) expresses, "Furthermore, because we are united with Christ, we have received an inheritance from God, for he chose us in advance, and he makes everything work out according to his plan."

Stay prayerful about everything—pray without ceasing, 1 Thessalonians 5:16 (KJV), even praying about: whose you are, who you are, what you want to become, and what visions and goals you have for the future. Put God first in everything, keep your eyes and drive headed toward your prize, and do not let anything distract or disrupt your plans, stay focused and intentional, and walk it out! Our race that God has graced us to partake of through life will include oppositions and opportunities to bring runners along while we run "to receive our prize" (1 Cor. 9:24–27, NIV). How we perceive tests and oppositions in life will determine our outcome; victory or defeat! Every one of us in the world is involved in this race of life, willingly or unwillingly, we are all involved, and need to know that God has chosen and purposed us to live an abundant life (John 10:10, KJV).

Before entering our race, let's get equipped to run a successful course! (Eph. 6) Wardrobe Department is calling all runners for an attire fitting. God has perfectly picked out the wardrobe, for all obedient, surrendered, true children of God. He has accurately fitted us with the whole armor of God that we would be able to stand against the tricks of the devil, one of our known enemies (Eph. 6:11, NIV). Unfortunately, we have a few more enemies that will show up in our race in life, as a matter of fact, in our very lane.

Those other enemies we need to be aware of, and stand against in prayer: for help and deliverance, are the world and our own flesh. We must know that at times in our spiritual walk, we become our own roadblock. God our Father who loves us so much has gifted us with the freedom of choice, and that ability to choose may lead us to use our freedom as an opportunity to follow the devil, and sin, as warned by 1 Peter 2:16 (ESV). Given the freedom of choice by the Lord himself, because of his love for us, should cause us to want to pursue right living with God, and maintain a character of integrity, honesty, and helpfulness.

Experiencing a greater chance at being an overcomer comes when we are apprised of distractions and tactics that may be used as attempts to derail us from our purpose and destiny. After stopping to get girded in the whole armor of od in Ephesians 6:10–18 (NIV), which includes, "Finally, be strong in the Lord and in his mighty power. Put on the full armor of God, so that you can stand against the devil's schemes. For our struggle is not against flesh and blood, but against the rulers, against the authorities, against the powers of this dark world, and against the spiritual forces of evil in the heavenly realms. Therefore put on the full armor of God, so that when the day of evil comes, you may be able to stand your ground, and after you have done everything to stand. Stand firm then, with the belt of truth buckled around your waist, with the breastplate of righteousness in place, and with your feet fitted with the readiness that comes from the gospel of peace. In addition to all this, take up the shield of faith, with which you can extinguish all the flaming arrows of the evil one. Take the helmet of salvation and the sword of the Spirit, which is the word of God. And pray in the Spirit on all occasions with all kinds of prayers and requests. With this in mind, be alert and always keep on praying for all the Lord's people." Our first prayer is to ask God to go before us, therefore, we are now ready to take our positions at the starting line.

Prior to the actual race beginning, "We must throw off everything that hinders, and the sin that so easily entangles, and let us run with perseverance, the race marked out for us . . . fixing our eyes on Jesus, the pioneer and finisher of faith" (Heb. 12:1–2 NIV). At times in life, our very attitude about ourselves could be a hindrance to running a victorious race. Success and productivity in our very existence are determined by our attitude as well. Taking the opportunity to be obedient, we need to steady our eyes on the one that has set the example of excellence for us to pattern our lives after. Jesus is the one to follow as reminded in 2 Peter 1:3 (ESV), as it states, "His divine power has granted to us all things that pertain to life and godliness, through the knowledge of him who called us to his own glory and excellence." Let me bless you with one more important component to assist you in your journey, you are already a winner. Even if we should experience a time where we feel we can't go on, God stands ready to carry us to the finish line. Set your precious minds on the thoughts that "I am a winner, and fully equipped to meet and overcome every obstacle that may try to derail or block my path."

Now that we have been physically and mentally prepared to move forward, knowing that we are more than conquerors; Runners, take your marks, wait! Did you remember to see if other runners are in their correct position to also run a victorious spiritual race? God has more than enough to reward all willing workers, who help build the kingdom of God with souls that we can aid others in their race, and still win. Our journey through life is not just about us receiving the prize, but everyone that comes to the saving knowledge of Jesus Christ. Okay, now runners take your marks, pray, get set, and go!

Each child of God, running the same race, often gets intertwined with other runners and our focus becomes blurred as we look at and listen to the voice of other runners. Intersecting other participants may at times cause us to clash. When we clash, boundary lines can become unclear, our focus gets off, and we can adopt an attitude of inability to finish our race for the prize, but that's when we need to pray harder and ask the Lord for his strength to finish the course laid out for us in his plan. Intentional, God-focused runners must also pay strict attention to warning signs in our path, especially if we do not know if those warning signs are signals for us. God our Father, who is so faithful, loving, and considerate sends warning signs for his children to keep us from falling into traps.

We may encounter warning signs such as Yield, Wrong Way, Stop, Merge, Slow Down, No U-Turn, and No Blocking Traffic, which could cause us to derail from our plans and even go down a destructive path, leading to a dead end. Have any of you ever thought that those street warning signs would be essential in our everyday spiritual walk? People, who I love, watch out particularly for those flashing warning signs because those signs signal impending danger. Some roads in life may appear to be safe, but there are dangers that are lurking around waiting to strip you of all that is vital to you being an impactful person in life, that's why we pray! All that is part of your life does not mean they are good for your life. My greatest oppositions in life have come by way of people who I thought loved me, at least, that's what they said. In the beginning of our relationships, that's even what it looked like, but then they made a detour, and I was left on the path to walk it alone, without physical companionship, but the Lord was always there with me.

In the midst of constant rejection and even abandonment, it is a battle to know you are still of great worth. Most of us have been in relationships with people that have turned their backs on us, for one reason or another, but life will and must go on. The hurt, brokenness, and anger that may arise from those times, offer us an out for healing, at least we are dealing with what has happened. Should we come to a crossroads in life, we must constantly remind ourselves to stay faithful, committed, and focused on the word of God and his plans for our lives. Jesus, himself, is an anchor in our Christian race if we keep holding on to him.

The anchor in a race is the one that brings up the rear, but it is also used to hold things steady, in place, which is desperately what we need. As I am sharing with you, I am learning how much the Lord loves and values each of us. There were times in my life where I wanted to ask the Lord Jesus where was he, when I was set up and could've been killed by drug dealers on numerous occasions trying to help my husband, not to be hurt, by them. There was no concern for my safety, when my husband called me to come bring him money because he needed it. There was no concern for me when I was pregnant and spotting and was left at home with no care for me or the baby's outcome. Thank God I didn't have to ask the Lord that question because he was right there with me through all that I went through, and the fact is he kept me safe and allowed my baby and I also to survive my spotting issue. I now say, "Now thanks be unto God which always causeth us to triumph in Christ, and maketh manifest the savour of his knowledge by us in every place" (2 Cor. 2:14 KJV). These are seasons when I developed a great trust in the Lord because I literally had no one else. Pressing into the word of God and asking God for help, I had to realize that I deserved better than what I was getting. I had to learn to value myself and stop accepting what was being handed to me and seek better.

"There is a time for everything, and a season for every activity under the heavens" (Eccles. 3:1, NIV). If we have not been made aware that each one of us has been purposed and destined, you have just been served notice! Since we do now know, that we were intentionally created, we don't have to be, "led astray and tossed to and fro and carried about with every wind of doctrine by the sleight of men and cunning craftiness, whereby they lie in wait to deceive" (Eph. 4:14, KJV). Regrettably, there are events and people that will affect our definition and worth of ourselves; however, recognizing that everyone we encounter in life will not have good intentions toward us. We must be confident in who we are, so that our identity will not fluctuate with every word someone verbalizes about us.

Our true identity comes from the one that created all living things, so it is up to us to search the scriptures to see what God says about his creation. It is vitally important for us to know who we are, and to be confident in it! I want to tell you about something that I was privileged to hear as I was struggling to know my worth. In my attempt to draw closer to the Lord, I went to a church function with my Hawaiian friend, Leilani, and during the testimony time, we were introduced to a little eight-year-old girl, who gave her testimony. The little girl went on to tell the audience that she was not planned or supposed to be here because her mother sought to abort her. Although, there she stood, on that auditorium stage in Whittier, California telling us to trust God and know that he is the giver of all life. That courageous little child said, "I had to fight to come to an understanding that I was of worth, planned and even wanted by the Lord and Savior, I had to also learn to forgive my mother for wanting to destroy me," those powerful life-changing words fell on all captive ears and eyes on that day. I can't remember if there were any dry eyes in the building, but I know my eyes were filled with tears. As the enemy tried to abort her purpose and destiny, to even have life, God said not so! In my spirit, I can hear the words of Job 33:4, NIV, as it states, "The spirit of God has made me; the breath of the Almighty gives me life." I would like to stand in the gap for all the unlearned, and apologize to all of you that may have dealt with hearing similar, hurtful, inconsiderate devastatingly cruel words from those who were supposed to love you! My heart goes out to you: the hurt and the broken, with prayers for healing of the wounds those words may have inflicted on you.

How many of you have been exposed to any depiction of a slavery movie? Even though we don't always get the just of what occurred in the true lives of slaves, movies try to give us a glimpse of the mistreatment of black people: physically, verbally, and emotionally, and sad to say those days are not gone. I am a descendant of slaves, tracing my dad's side of the family back to a kinfolk who signed up on a slave ship as a young servant girl. Interested in my family roots caused me to search more thoroughly into where my family came from. Reading about slave treatment has also made me more sensitive to the treatment of all people. Dealing with vicious people, most of my life, has caused me to desire to treat others better than I had been treated. For some reason, I became a target for verbal abuse because I was basically a quiet person. Verbal abuse was not just limited to people I did not know, but it even came by way of people that were supposed to love me. Though late in life I learned that verbally abusive people are not sure of their own worth, so they belittle others to make themselves look or feel better about who they are. I don't know about any of you but knowing that others feel bad about themselves, brings very little comfort to healing the hurt places those degrading words caused.

What's really sad is verbal abuse, physical abuse, and emotional abuse are not just being done to black people, now. Everyone is being attacked, by that enemy, which comes to steal kill and destroy as he is wreaking havoc in our land in John 10:10 (KJV). There is an everyday battle to not succumb to what is being said or done to us. Keeping our mouths closed or closing our eyes does not make the inhumane, ugly, wicked conduct go away, we must effectively deal with all troubling situations immediately, so roots of anger, hatred, bitterness, unforgiveness, vengeance, or resentment won't take hold in our lives, killing our potential to be witnesses of the love of God. Everything we do in life for others should be based on love!

If at any time, we get caught up in a mindset of everything is fair game, we are on a destructive course. Have you ever encountered anyone that has used these words on you, "I'm grown and I can do and say what I want to?" If you've encountered one such selfish person, I pray that you prayed and asked God to strip that spirit of inconsideration off of that uncaring person! Each time I hear those words, it's like someone sticks a knife in my heart because that person shows a lack of concern for others. Philippians 2:3 (NIV) states, "Do nothing out of selfish ambition or vain conceit. Rather, in humility value others above yourselves." If by chance we are one of those persons that walk according to the statement, "we are grown," then we are not walking in alignment with the word of God, therefore, we are being disobedient.

Sometimes in life, we veer off course and have to fight to get back on track! The year 2020 opened up a time for all the world to fight back when the world was thrown a curve ball with the corona virus. Some people believe that 2020 ushered in the year of the mask, but I beg to differ with that opinion because a lot of us have been wearing masks way before 2020. Various situations in life have caused us to mask who we are! In mankind's strong desire to want to fit in and even belong, we mask up to be like other people. Check this out; we dress like people intentionally, we get hairstyles like others on purpose, and we will allow others to dictate to us what to wear. Where did we disappear to in these times?

In our desires to be accepted, we will go as far as to allow this to happen, someone tells you, "I don't like what you have on," and you will go back in the house and change into another outfit, to try to satisfy the inconsiderate one who made that comment. Skipping back in the house, and putting on a different outfit solved what? Was your new mask and outfit sufficient, or did you have to jump through another hoop to make them feel good about, how you look? You just put on another mask to make you look the way he/she wanted you to look. What is so funny to me is that people have a picture in their heads as to how you can look better. Two scenarios come to mind regarding my looks, one man got perturbed at me because I did not wear lipstick to highlight my lips that he thought were sensual, and another man, as we sat in the moonlight, gazing into one another's eyes, he told me, "I better not catch you wearing makeup because you don't need it." Two different viewpoints about the same person, who will you listen to or are you able to make your own choice, for what works for you? Time to unmask and be who God intentionally made you to be!

All of us can agree that the 2020 pandemic threw the whole world off guard causing us to leave behind what always worked for us. The Lord promised that "he would never leave us or forsake us" (Heb. 13:5, KJV). The Lord will be with us through heartaches, troubles, deaths, viruses, pandemics, tornadoes, earthquakes, hurricanes, and any and all natural disasters! For those of you who may not know; we are only here today because of the Lord's faithfulness, forgiveness, friendship, favor, love, mercy, and grace. God our father has kissed us this day and allowed us to run on while tasting of his goodness, awakening us to his love, partaking of his daily bread, and giving us the ability to live and have our being (Acts 17:28, ESV). Knowing that, "The earth is the Lord's, and the fullness thereof; the world, and they that dwell therein" (Ps. 24:1, KJV), should leave us comforted, that the things that may try to place a value on us on earth can't compare to the value that the one who created us puts on us.

Critics of who we are vary because there are always folks who want to have a say in who we are or should become in life, just because they can see us! No one has to be invited to comment about your life, everyone is just openly opinionated these days! Included in our defining process, as we move through life, is the world and all that it entails, things that we've experienced in life, and of course, the one, who, fearfully and wonderfully made us as stated in Psalm 139:14 (KJV). It is primarily up to us to decide, who we permit to weigh in on defining our usefulness.

In our fight to maintain confidence in our worth, let's stack the fight in our favor. First, we must know what we ourselves have to offer anyone, so we need to spend time alone and ask ourselves what do I possess that make people want to spend time in my presence? Next, look into the mirror of the word of God, and see if we have any traits that cause us to look like Jesus. Finally, follow after what is right and do good! Become a magnet for change, and raise the standard for all who come your way, showing them how to be the best, positive, life-changing, impactful people possible. Philippians 4:8 (NIV) gives us a direction to help us in having a healthy attitude and thought process as it states, "Finally, brothers and sisters, whatever is true, whatever is noble, whatever is right, whatever is pure, whatever is lovely, whatever is admirable—if anything is excellent or praiseworthy—think about such things." If all the world would walk in those key areas, we would not have to defend ourselves in the world as much, but anyway! The process of working to have a healthy attitude and mindset may very well begin in us, God's children.

We must be aware that we will come across people that are just, wicked, who have their own deceptive plans for us and will label us calling us all sorts of names, but we mustn't allow those abusive names to stick with us. Philippians 4:8 gives me a place of refuge to return to when I encounter verbally abusive folk. I let those words marinate in my heart that I will not become what I despise. Learning in life and through teaching, that we learn by repetition, whether positive or negative actions, we must be cautious on what we frequently display for eyes are always on us. When behaviors are repeated and we don't have moral or spiritual standards in place, we act out behaviors that have often been exhibited in our lives. Having been in ministry for a long time, I've interacted with many people: some hurt, abused, angry, broken, and even suicidal, learning through conversation that some of them have developed the same characteristics as the ones that hurt them. Being careful what we feed ourselves is essential for what goes in will come out! Just like children that sit in the presence of older people all the time, they start acting like they've been here before, but they're just being sponges of who was around them the most.

At this moment, take time to look in a real mirror and ask yourself as you behold your face in the mirror, who am I? What do you really see when you look in the mirror, is it all the flaws you have or the good qualities you possess? You may even replay in your mind one of the worst verbal attacks you've been involved in. The answers may vary because it will depend on who we have allowed to speak over us at the time. Maturing and growing in our walk opens to us more areas that may impact our defining process. Thinking about this personally reminds me that we are identified by our appearance, friends, behavior, family, finances, accomplishments, and at times our name. Try this on with me and see if this is a perfect fit for you as well, incidence that has occurred in your life has caused you to feel a certain way about yourself. How about this, each one of your immediate family members worked in your dad's company, every one of them but you! Where does that leave you in your opinion of yourself? Previously mentioned entities are important in our lives, but yet, we let them have too much control over who we are or what we develop into.

Would I be correct in saying that females, especially, need to know their own worth before we can believe someone else's value of us? Luke 12:7 (NIV) enlightens us to the fact that "Indeed, the very hairs of your head are all numbered. Don't be afraid; you are worth more than many sparrows." Picture someone loving you enough to care about the number of hairs on your head, that's God! If we get direction and affirmation from the one that created us as a masterpiece, then we will experience this walk in life in a more worthwhile way including knowing that you are valuable even if every one of your siblings were born in the month of December, leaving you the odd ball once again!

Should we look at God as one who makes no mistakes, then we'll possibly be able to stop playing hide-n-seek with individuals. We play hide-n-seek when we don't want people to know what we are really like. If we accept God's freedom from entering the game of hide-n-seek, we'll be able to freely walk in and utilize all the gifts and talents the Lord has placed down in us causing us to be a light of godly impact on all the Lord brings in our realm of influence.

God, in the beginning, said, "Let us make man in our image and likeness" (Gen. 1:26, KJV), and I often wonder what all that encompasses, but what I do know is it involves having confidence in what the Trinity (the Father, the Son, and the Holy Spirit) created. Are we willing to adopt that same confidence that the Trinity spoke over us that if we become involved in vicious mudslinging and verbal abuse, we will know how to encourage ourselves with the word of God? Even when we confidently know we have a lot to offer or to benefit others through the work the Lord has done on us, we still shy away from engagement. This is the time when we need to affirm ourselves. "For we are his workmanship (masterpiece), created in, Christ Jesus, unto good works" (Eph. 2:10, KJV), so let us maintain that mindset throughout life, regardless of what may befall us!

Do not be fooled to think I am only speaking to you since oftentimes, I am met with the same dilemma because most of the people I have close relationships with are older than I, so I tend to hold back what the Lord has allowed me to come to the knowledge of by the spirit of God, through studying the word of

God. Because many believe wisdom comes through old age, we need to listen to the words of Elihu, the son of Barakel, the Buzite from Job 32:6–10 (NIV), when he utters these words, "I am young in years, and you are old; that is why I was fearful, not daring to tell you what I know. I thought, 'Age should speak; advanced years should teach wisdom.' But it is the spirit in a person, the breath of the Almighty that gives them understanding. It is not only the old who are wise, not only the aged who understand what is right. Therefore I say: Listen to me; I too will tell you what I know." Blessed by the wise words of Elihu, I am more willing to share the words of understanding the Lord has allowed me to acquire. God has even graced me with an audience that now wants to grow in the knowledge of the Lord and Savior, Jesus Christ, regardless of my age. The women's ministry at New Horizon Missionary Baptist Church of Lynwood, California, is one welcoming ministry that I am able to pour the word of God into, studying with older individuals. God has awesomely graced me to teach a zoom Bible class with mixed ages on the call on Sundays. A surrendered, submitted, committed, obedient, child of God will walk through, some only God-opened doors.

When God blesses you to be an incubator of change, you may encounter a lonely walk, depending on your family and friends' perception of your hunger to please the Lord and be obedient to his call on your life. Your journey to pursue better and what is right may cause you to be left out of a lot of activities that does not fit what your future looks like. In the quiet places, as I laid prostrate before the Lord, I was truly able to hear God and experience his power and revelation word. In the quiet is a true test of you maintaining your focus on your goals and not relaxing your standards to fit in and belong. "We can do all things through Christ who strengthens us" (Phil. 4:13, KJV)!

Our confidence and direction come from spending time alone in the presence of the one that took the time to uniquely make us. Serving a God that has purposed and destined each of his children gives us a path that we should follow that leads us to Jesus and eternal life. Romans 8:27 (NLT) and Psalm 139:1–6 (KJV) should put our minds at ease to know we are loved and that he knows us better than we know ourselves. I am further reminded that Jesus loved us so much that he gave his life (John 3:16, KJV), as a sacrifice to pay the penalty for our sins. Jesus saw something in us worth dying for, so he did! Give a listen, on YouTube, to Anthony Brown and group therapy, singing "Worth" from their album, *Everyday Jesus,* as they walk you through what the Lord Jesus did for all he loved and who will accept and believe it.

On the road to knowing our worth, we must carefully examine Psalm 139:14 (KJV) which declares, "We are fearfully and wonderfully made and we know right well." It is truly a process in rising to the fact of knowing we are fearfully and wonderfully made. Ridicule and hardships unfold in our lives, and if we don't know the character of the Lord, we could believe like some that he does not like us because he allows us to go through troubles in life. There are tests the Lord allows to come across our path to work out a far greater outcome in us; to develop our character and to train us in maintaining godly integrity. Taking the time to intentionally study the word of God on the attributes and character of God lead me to a calming place in the Lord that showed me that even in my disobedient state, he still speaks the same of me, and his agape love for me does not waver!

I miss my grandpa, Otis (odes) hart, he would call me from Arkansas and say, "Hello good lookin', what you got cookin'?" His words always brought a smile to my face and laughter to my voice.

He was one that I knew loved me as I was. Should any of you be like me, you need more assurance on your worth in life! This area of knowing my worth has been a hard battle for me. I've basically been a quiet person, most of my life, and people have mistaken my meekness for weakness and chose to bully, degrade, belittle, take advantage of, and make attempts at publicly humiliating me that I am so done with it! I don't know if any of you have been turned on, by folks who were your friends, well I have. I've had people who tried to set me up to be hurt, abused, and could have been killed. What is so hard to believe is that they were people who had been in my life for years. Be alert, all that smile in your face could be plotting behind your back. I had to encourage myself to know I deserve better, and must maintain the posture the Lord has given me to still reach out and help all I can. I thank God that even in my brokenness, I still have a desire to try to make life better for Gods' people.

Being able to believe and receive compliments from others takes me some time to accept now. It often takes an overriding and washing by the word of God to clear my thoughts of verbally abusive words said to me, and the physical intentional hurt done to me; this is the time when I submerge myself in the word of God, reading the word of God out loud so the words will be absorbed in my hearing ears, and then I incorporate those words in prayer back to the Lord, God my father, who is always ready to hear the cries of his children. God will handle all the people who have abused you and me! In my pursuit of the Lord, I ask him to cleanse me, purify my thoughts, and wash me with his word bringing me to a place of healing and wholeness. If we do not immediately deal with what's been negatively or hurtfully done to us, we may develop deadly roots, which bears repeated warning because those roots can grow fruit, which will look nothing like the character of Jesus. If we do not acknowledge what was done to us and release it to the Lord or whomever your outlet person is, then once the roots begin to grow, they become hard to get rid of! The fruit of those roots and the damage done may be unrecognizable, but we know something is wrong because we do not speak or walk the way we use to.

At times it seems so sad that our own worth is determined by the viewpoint of other people, but we can fix that if we listen more to what God says concerning us than mankind. Remembering God can not lie (Heb. 6:18, ESV), so let's hold to his words over us. In our quest for wanting to fit in and belong, we forget Gods' plan for his sons and daughters, according to Psalm 4:3 (ESV), which states, "Know that the Lord has set apart the godly for himself . . ." From the beginning, our father had an awesome plan for our lives! Jeremiah 29:11–13 helps us in this area, even though it was to the exiles from Jerusalem that were carried into Babylon, I believe the words are pertinent today. Jeremiah 29:11–13 (NIV) says, "'For I know the plans I have for you,' declares the Lord, 'plans to prosper you and not to harm you, plans to give you hope and a future. Then you will call on me and come and pray to me, and I will listen to you. You will seek me and find me when you seek me with all your heart." What an open door of love, care, concern, faithfulness, compassion, and victory! In tears, right now, recalling how faithful God has been to me. Allowing me to experience his awesome plans in my life, when it looked like the enemy was going to win.

If God in all his holiness thinks well of us, what does it really matter what the world, the devil, friends or family thinks about us. Let's encourage one another with, 1 Peter 2:9 (NIV), where it declares, "But you are a chosen people, a royal priesthood, a holy nation, God's special possession, that you may declare the praises of him who called you out of darkness into his wonderful light." What a way to be defined by God, who lets us know that we have been titled, positioned, and directed in our path in life if we humbly surrender to his deliberately laid out plans, for all who will obediently follow him. In 1 Peter 2:9, I see that these are some of the very things we fight against in life, but not realizing that's how God made us to be, set apart, different, noble, royal, and grateful expressers of the works he has done. As we are still at work unmasking ourselves, let's start accepting all the good and perfect gifts the Lord has for us (Ja. 1:17, KJV). Read Deuteronomy 28 in your set aside time to get to know the Lord and allow him to speak into you as you find out other blessings the Lord has in store for those who believe and walk in obedience to his will for their lives.

I pray that you are being affirmed in the Lord as I am as we learn how much we are really loved and how valuable we are in the Lord's eyes. Romans 5:8 says, "But God demonstrates his own love for us in this: While we were still sinners, Christ died for us." We were not even attempting to walk in right standing with God, nor at any time focusing on him, but he in his awesomeness, was focused on us, "working things out for our good" (Rom. 8:28, KJV).

Brothers and sisters, is it all right for us to move on up a little more, from the thinking phase to the knowing phase? Relax a moment in Psalm 139, chill there for help! Psalm 139:1–5 uplifts us with these words, "O Lord you have searched me and known me! You know when I sit down and when I rise up; you discern my thoughts from afar. You search out my path and my lying down and are acquainted with all my ways. Even before a word is on my tongue, behold, O Lord you know it altogether. You hem me in, behind and before, and lay your hand upon me." How powerful and comforting are the words of Psalm 139:1–5 to the true worshippers of God. I don't know if you can see love in this passage, but I do. When you love someone, you want to know everything about the one you love and that is what God has said to us, "I love you and want to know every detail of your life, as you verbally invite me in, to have my way."

Grasp this open invitation as our longsuffering, kind, generous, forgiving, merciful, savior allows us the opportunity to know him as our provider, deliverer, and healer in our lives. Are you willing to open yourselves up to receive his outpouring of love, in and on you? His love can work in you to change anything that is not like God in you and on you so that you may be able to minister in love to all the Lord brings your way. This time, why not knowingly surrender to God our father, seeing as he has been working on our behalf even when we did not recognize him. I guarantee if you look back over your life, you can now see God's hand of mercy that was upon you because things could have turned out so much worse, but God!

Going back down memory lane, I was able to see God's protective hand on my life. Recalling a time when I and some friends attended a Pasadena vacant house party and I was Invited to dance, so I left my refreshment on the counter, where I was standing and went to dance. We danced to one of the longest songs in history, so it seemed. After the long enjoyable dance, I returned to attempt to hydrate myself with my drink, but someone picked up my drink before I did, and as he began drinking the soda, he started acting very strange. He started playing the bar as a piano, wailing his legs in the air and saying crazy things. A little later, came to find out, by my personal bodyguard that someone laced my drink with something. Are you seeing how that could've been me, out of my mind, or even dead? I saw God at work, rescuing me even back then! For someone to love us even when we didn't know him is making a great statement of care, worth, and unconditional (godly) love!

God's love is so awesome, steady, and available to all who want to tap into what he offers. Gods' love at work in us can open doors for us to be blessings in the lives of others! Matthew 22:39 (NIV) says . . . love your neighbor as yourself. Leviticus 19:18 (ESV), states, "Forget about the wrong things people do to you; don't try to get even. Love your neighbor as yourself. I am the Lord." These two scriptures seem so easy to understand on the surface, but can we explore another aspect of these passages? The Lord our creator is here affirming who we are, for if he did not see worth in us, he would not tell us to love anyone else the way we love ourselves. These two scriptures actually blessed my heart because so many times people have said some very unkind, less than flattering words to me that would have rendered me unable to effectively operate according to those commands, but God! If God had not encouraged my soul in his word, I would have been really messed up because the Lord also teaches us that "we are to go and make disciples of all nations" (Matt. 28:19, KJV).

In order for the children of God to effectively discharge the duty of making disciples, we need to become grounded in the word of God. We must not only know the word of God, but we must walk according to it and maintain a standard of integrity, by being obedient to the word of God, at all times. What we use to disciple others is totally based on what the word of God says. Taking our cues from the Lord himself, we will stay on course and walk in confidence and victory more times than not! Allowing God to lead us will give all of us the opportunity to be spiritually healthy and whole as we walk this race together, in unity, helping each other to succeed. Keeping Jesus as our example of excellence, we will experience life how God intended for us to taste of it. In John 10:10 (ESV) scripture says, "The thief comes only to steal and kill and destroy. I came that they may have life and have it abundantly." The Lord Jesus in his love and care for us continues to warn us about oppositions we may face in life, Jesus also stands ready to fight for us and to bring us through.

Knowing your worth through the identity of the word leads us back to Psalm 139, but this time, let's put our eyes on verses 13–14, where it announces, "For You formed my inward parts; You covered me in my mother's womb. I will praise You, for I am fearfully and wonderfully made; Marvelous are your works, And that my soul knows very well" (Ps. 139:13–14, NKJV). Sons and daughters of God, and sons and daughters of God's children, keep this in mind as we journey on through knowing our worth: we are the Lord's masterpiece!

I hope you remember that 1 Peter 2:9 says you are of royal lineage, so now it's time for you to put on your royal attire, and meet me at the royal gates of the palace of the citadel in Susa from the book of Esther. You should already have on the whole armor of God from Ephesians 6:10–18 (NIV), so now all you need to do is put on your royal robe or cloak to be ready for the festivities that we'll be attending. We should be adequately equipped to attend the party at the palace, even if we encounter uninvited guests who always like to disrupt good plans and more so, God's plans.

Now that we are all present and accounted for, let's go meet King Ahasuerus and Queen Vashti, our royal hosts. They have prepared a celebration in honor of the victories they have accomplished working together in Susa. This feast was for the nobles, officials, the military leaders of Persia, and media and the princes and nobles of the 127 provinces the king ruled over, wow, and they were all in attendance. Hold on to your eyeballs and stomachs because this banquet was to last for 180 days. King Ahasuerus, Queen Vashti, and only the nobles of the provinces of the citadel of Susa had a party of splendor and majesty for days on end. That celebration finally came to an end, but the celebrating is not done by far! Still, in the book of Esther, chapter 1 (ESV), we see another party about to jump off, this time for seven glorious days.

Come with me to the garden, no not the one where it says "the garden alone" because this time, it's going to be a group of folks banqueting in the king's enclosed garden in the palace. Gorgeously decorated with silver, gold, and purple, the people from the least to the greatest that lived in the citadel were invited to the festivities this time. There was a royal spread set out, just as before, but this time, there was an unlimited open wine bar included at the disposal of the attendees. Queen Vashti was also hosting a banquet for the women in a separate location from where the king was hosting, the men who had access to an unlimited supply of wine.

Let's peek in on the women in queen Vashti's banquet going on in the palace. I'm sure they too had wine, but not as much as was made available to the men. All I can imagine the women doing is eating and talking to one another about the mundane things happening around the palace. The women could be sharing stories about how it is to be part of the royal line because all of those in attendance were not part of the upper class. Well, as days rolled on and the men were quite tipsy and high in spirit, the king had a bright idea to call for his wife, Queen Vashti, who was very lovely to look upon, to come and show off herself in front of a group of wine drunk men.

King Ahasuerus sent some men to fetch queen Vashti to come model before the group of wasted men, and queen Vashti in her love for herself refused to open the door to what could have been a harmful situation for her. Queen Vashti had more respect and value for herself than to put herself in danger, to please a husband, a king, and or a high spirited man. I see queen Vashti as a strong woman, who knew her worth and I too believe she was prepared for what would follow by not obeying the kings' request. Esther chapter 1 (ESV), will give you a detailed account of all that transpired with queen Vashti, take a read for yourself. How would any of you have handled the same scenario?

Knowing that queen Vashti had a hard decision to make: to lose her position in the palace or lose her self-respect and worth of herself, she made it nonetheless. Queen Vashti walked away with her virtue, self-respect, and dignity intact. I don't know about you, but when I face hard times and need to be comforted, I run to gospel music and listen to songs on YouTube like Helen Baylor's "Wounded Soldier," Mervin Mayo's "You Know My Name" and "What Kind of Man" to help get my focus and mindset back in the right place to not dwell on what I'd been through. I can't forget Donald Lawrence and the Tri-City Singers' "I Am God" because if you are ever in need of comfort or assurance of God in your life, pull up Donald Lawrence and the Tri-City Singers, and bless yourself. If for any reason you need more to encourage yourself, take a listen to Jason Nelson's song, "Forever."

It is so befitting to learn our worth from the one who bestowed our worth on us as he knows his worth as well. Isaiah 46:9–10

(ESV) says, "Remember the former things of old; for I am God, and there is no other; I am God and there is none like me . . ." getting confidence from the one that gives confidence is so great because we will be able to stay on the right track learning from the best. Isaiah 45:22 (NIV) also helps us with knowing our God as it states, "Turn to me and be saved, all the ends of the earth! For I am God, and there is no other."

I pray you enjoyed your short stay at the royal feasts, I also pray you to know that you belonged in the presence of royalty for we are the king of kings' kids! We must now travel on in search of more clarity and vision tuning. Join me as we are taken captive with the Hebrew boys who were taken from their homeland in Judah and carried to Babylon. These young men were stripped from all they knew and put in a strange place to perform tasks that were thrust upon them. In the book of Daniel (KJV), we find these Hebrew boys: Daniel, Mishael, Azariah, and Hananiah, who were being held captive and made to submit to new authority. These young men were not only taken captive: their names were changed, their daily regimen was altered, and they had to fight to maintain their character and love for the God of Israel, rulers tried to force them to eat food from the king's table, to which they were not accustomed, but they maintained their own food staple and were more fit than those that ate from the king's table. Before we go any further, I must let you know that we know these men as Belteshazzar (Daniel), the very Daniel of the lion's den, and the other three men: Shadrach (Hananiah), Meshach (Mishael) and Abednego (Azariah) are the Hebrew boys that were thrown in the fiery furnace. These God-selected men knew that they were specially selected by God to carry out his mission to save others. The hand of the Lord and his divine favor was upon these men as they stood up in obedience to what God had called them to do, even at the threat of losing their lives. These men, in all that they experienced in the book of Daniel, remained faithful to God knowing that the Lord was right there with them and had always been working in their lives. Are we able to stand with the Hebrew boys knowing that God is always with us? These God-chosen, courageous men refused to bow to any other entity or to give up what they knew worked in their lives.

To know your worth and to know God loved you enough to see you through whatever turmoil would befall you means you are of great value to our father, God. This sure held true for my son Zaire, when he was having transition problems when first starting school. I comforted my son and told him, "Mommy can't be with you always, but the Lord Jesus can." He went to school with no further issues and he excelled and is still excelling in the power of the Lord. Parents who love the Lord with all their heart should pass that along to their children even while in the womb, giving them a great foundation and a head start in this uncertain world. By the way, the Hebrew boys we talked about were young men when they started their journey in Babylon, some even say they were in their teen years. Does that spark any drive in you to hold to God's promises and trust and believe he is always with us?

It is seen and often said by people who recognize their times of testing that one's true character is revealed and other character developed in testing times. Queen Vashti, Zaire, Daniel, Shadrach, Meshach, and Abednego in the trials they were permitted to experience; exercised godly character showing that true character is definitely exposed when you are in the line of fire, only if your foundation was sure and right from your beginning. When you spend time in the presence of greatness, there is a great possibility that greatness is planted in you, and if nurtured, and trained the traits will be manifested.

Being constantly reminded of God's love for us is a joy in this walk of life! If you have ever taken time to look back over troubles that came your way, were you blessed to recognize the power of God aiding you through every one of them? "The steadfast love of the Lord never ceases; his mercies never come to an end; they are new every morning; great is your faithfulness"(Lam. 3:22–23, ESV). There is something else that we need to always keep in the forefront of our minds, and that is, we are in a race to finish the course the Lord has predestined for us. We are instructed to tell all we come in contact with, about our Lord and Savior Jesus Christ, and to strive to receive our prize, and to know our purpose and reach our destiny. In our race, we may face many detours, some derailments, and the need for repositioning if we do not remain focused and intentional on allowing God to go before us and make our way straight.

Running on, come with me to the valley of Sorek in the book of Judges, chapter 16(NIV), where we will meet the Philistine woman, Ms. Delilah and her beau, mighty warrior, Judge Samson, the Israelite. Samson the mighty man always dibbled and dabbled in a culture he shouldn't have had any dealings with. As a man set apart for God's purpose, Samson had some guidelines he was supposed to adhere to, but he chose to do things his own way. Don't laugh, doesn't that sound like some of us? Samson was in a constant battle with the Philistines, but yet he so loved Philistine women! Samson, once again, caught in a web behind a Philistine woman, this time, Delilah was out to put this strong warrior out of commission for the money they offered her, and to help her people, the Philistines. Delilah used her seductive powers: her smooth, persuasive, peaceful soft voice, her repetitive asking, and her cozy, comfy lap to coerce Samson to divulge the source of his strength. I believe that this is a good time to warn women that we are part Delilah, which part you are. I'm leaving it up to you! As I sit in my living room laughing because I would love to hear some responses from some of the women as to what part of Delilah they possess. Delilah was working her persuasive, sex-appealed plan on Samson causing him to forget his purpose in life, lose focus, drop his guard possibly forgetting his name, becoming side-tracked, leaving him smooth-talked, caressed, and coerced out of telling the source of his power. Believing Delilah loved him and had his best interest in his heart, he caved into the satisfaction of fleshly desires and got deceived. Samson, who had been personally set apart for the work of the Lord's plan, threw away his purpose and yielded to temporary pleasures. Samson was not even aware that his enemies were close by, waiting to capture him. Once the Philistines heard the source of his strength, they pounced on Samson cutting off his hair, which was his power source, given to him by God, who had set him apart for his use.

Samson's strength was no longer as his hair was cut off by the Philistines, he was tied up, eyes put out, and he was taken and bound to pillars and mocked by all. Samson became the entertainment for a Philistine party. During his time of captivity, his hair began to grow back. Samson's new hair growth allowed a portion of his strength to return, which was unnoticed by the Philistines. While the Philistine party was in full effect, Samson being blind was able to feel his way between two pillars, and with all his might, and the power of God in action, he pushed those pillars loose causing the structure to collapse, killing all in attendance, which was more than he had killed in his time of living. The book of Judges will give you a greater look at Samson and his walk as a mighty man. For the children of God and the world that will receive this lesson, the Lord is yet showing us how loved we are as he warns us to be prayerful, watchful, and alert in our journey through every day! He also shows us his mercy and forgiveness when we are the messed-up culprits!

Opening the door to our last biblical travel stop, I ask that you would put on your prayer robe and pray and intercede for all women that may be involved in a similar walk to our next witness. In the word of God, the Lord so graciously allows us to see a glimpse of ourselves, so that we will know that the word of God will work for us as well. We will find this door as we travel to the hill country of Ephraim in the book of 1 Samuel, chapter 1. Let's walk and see the sights that the Lord has splendidly wrought for all creation to enjoy. As we reach the door to the home of Elkanah, an Ephrathite, who had two wives Peninnah and Hannah, I will unlock the door for us to go in with the key that I have around my neck that I hold close to my heart. In this home, we will first meet Peninnah, the woman that had several children and taunted her husband's other wife who had no children. Peninnah always made time to make Hannah aware of her barrenness, which caused Hannah great hurt. Being barren was tearing Hannah apart, and she could not bear it any longer. Hannah had to be one heck of a woman, and definitely aware of what she had to offer to even stay committed in that type of relationship; Hannah was sharing her husband with another woman and unable to have any children by him. Both of those women had to be some kind of special to be able to coexist in that type of family structure.

The family had yearly journeys to worship and sacrifice to the Lord of Hosts in Shiloh, and Elkanah would take the time to give portions to his family. He gave to Peninnah and all her sons and daughters; and to Hannah, he gave a worthy portion because she didn't have any children. During these trips and blessing times, Peninnah took a special interest in making Hannah feel worse about her being childless. Elkanah saw the grief of his wife Hannah and could not do anything to fill the void she was experiencing, but he tried. In being backed into a no way out situation, Hannah began to fight in a different way, she took it to the Lord God Almighty. The family was on their trip to worship the Lord, and Hannah left from where the family was and went into a solitary place to pour her heart and desires out to the Lord. With no distractions, she did like Philippians 4:6–7 (NKJV) tells us, "Be anxious for nothing, but in everything by prayer and supplication, with thanksgiving, let your requests be made known to God; and the peace of God which surpasses all understanding, will guard your hearts and minds through Christ Jesus." Hannah stood in the Lord's presence and bore all to him, letting him know all she felt: from her reproach for not having a child, to her feeling left out, and less than other women especially her husband's other wife. Hannah could have also been telling God that "I am thankful for what you have given me, but father God, I am facing feelings of emptiness and longing to have a child to pour my love into and to teach about your love." She could have gone as far as to tell him, "Father, this is my heart's desire and I know that you are the giver of life, so please look on me and bless me at this time."

Now that I have snuck in a glimpse of what I went through, let's see what Hannah did in her approach to God. 1 Samuel 1:10–17, NIV, "In her deep anguish Hannah prayed to the Lord, weeping bitterly. She made a vow, saying, 'Lord Almighty, if you will only look on your servant's misery and remember me, and not forget your servant, but give her a son, then I will give him to the Lord for all the days of his life, and no razor will ever be used on his head.' As she kept on praying to the Lord, Eli observed her mouth. Hannah was praying in her heart, and her lips were moving but her voice was not heard. Eli thought she was drunk and said to her, 'How long are you going to stay drunk? Put away your wine.' 'Not so my Lord,' Hannah replied, 'I am a woman who is deeply troubled. I have not been drinking wine or beer; I was pouring out my soul to the Lord. Do not take your servant for a wicked woman; I have been praying here out of my anguish and grief.' Eli answered, 'Go in peace and may the God of Israel grant you what you asked of him.'"

Thank God that as Hannah trusted God with all her heart and leaned not to her own understanding in all her ways acknowledging him, he directed her path (Prov. 3:5–6, KJV). Awesome, mighty God was on the move again in the life of a surrendered child. Hear 1 Samuel 1:19, (NIV), "Early the next morning they arose and worshiped before the Lord and then went back to their home at Ramah. Elkanah made love to his wife Hannah, and the Lord remembered her." Take a blessed walkthrough to 1 and 2 Samuel as you recognize the mighty move of God in how he answered Hannah's earnest petitions and how God turned things around in her life including all that the enemy meant for evil. God worked all things out for her good (Rom. 8:28, KJV), hallelujah!

Is God taking you to a solitary place to be alone in his presence that he may speak life into you as he visions you and helps you to realize that you are purposed, loved, and cared for? Absent from distractions, God's able to get our attention easier, so he can tell us that we are special to him, and he's ready willing, and able to answer our earnest pleas. I mentioned to you earlier in the book that all my siblings were born in December, but what I did not tell you is that all of them were born in the twenties in December like they were planned, and even my two sisters' names are similar in ending spelling. Can you imagine that those oddball feelings made me run even harder to find out where I fit in, in life? It was already hard, being a middle child; never being called my oldest, or my baby, so I worked harder to become more than they saw me as. I had to convince myself that I was more than just a misfit in my family, so I sought the Lord for affirmation and approval for who I was and still for who I am in him. I have a little secret for you, anytime someone told me what I could not do, I sought with all that was in me to prove them wrong. I've always been compared to other people, and I never measured up to the ones I was compared to, so I sought my own identity to find my own worth and abilities. This also gave me the heart to be an encourager to all I can, a supporter to all that stand in need, and help to all God sends my way.

In the power of the excellence of his love, God truly desires, we would know that all he made is good, and in the midst of everything we may go through in life, he will be there with us for he promised he would never leave us or forsake us according to Deuteronomy 31:6 (NIV) and Hebrews 13:5 (ESV). Knowing the love of God from the earliest existence of our birth and well before we were placed in our mother's wombs is so marvelous to know. We were thought about before the world was created! "Even before he made the world, God loved us and chose us in Christ to be holy and without fault in his eyes" (Eph. 1:4, NLT). Putting the extra seal on the thoughts of our value of ourselves, remembering to take our cue from our creator, we marinate in these words from Psalm 139:15–16, (ESV), "My frame was not hidden from you, when I was being made in secret, intricately woven in the depths of the earth. Your eyes saw my unformed substance; in your book were written, every one of them, the days that were formed for me, when as yet there was none of them."

Brothers and sisters, sons and daughters of God, know you are of worth, know your worth, love who you are, and know that God made you and loves you! Don't stop growing, seeking God, walking upright, and bettering yourself in the Lord. Commit yourself unto the Lord, trust also in him and he shall bring it to pass (Ps. 37:5). God can make you better than you could ever imagine as you trust his plans for your life. Isaiah 53:1 questions our mindsets asking, "Whose report will you believe?"

DEFINING MOMENTS
NAVIGATIONAL STRATEGIES

a. Accept—Deuteronomy 7:9 (KJV), "Know therefore that the Lord thy God, he is God, the faithful God, which keepeth the covenant and mercy to them that love him and keep his commandments through a thousand generations;"

c. Confess—"Therefore confess your sins to each other and pray for each other so that you may be healed. The prayer of a righteous person is powerful and effective" (Ja. 5:16, NIV).

f. Forgive—Romans 12:17 (NIV), "Do not repay anyone evil for evil. Be careful to do what is right in the eyes of everyone."

p. Pray—"Do not be anxious about anything, but in every situation, by prayer and petition, with thanksgiving, present your requests to God. And the peace of God, which transcends all understanding, will guard your hearts and your minds in Christ Jesus" (Phil. 4:6–7, NIV).

r. Remember—Titus 2:14 (ESV), ". . . our great God and savior Jesus Christ, gave himself for us to redeem from lawlessness and to purify for himself a people for his own possession, who are zealous for good works."

t. Teach—"Show yourself in all respects to be a model of good works and in your teaching show integrity, dignity, and sound speech that cannot be condemned, so that an opponent may be put to shame, having nothing evil to say about us" (Titus 2:7–8, NIV).

w. Walk it out—Colossians 1:10–11 (NIV), "So that you may live a life worthy of the Lord and please him in every way: bearing fruit in every good work, growing in the knowledge of God, being strengthened with all power according to his glorious might so that you may have great endurance and patience."

Defining moments
Whose report will you believe?

Prayer focus:

1. Pray that you would recognize that defining moments can also come through positive compliments.

2. You would develop a heart for others.

3. That you would trust God to protect and keep you from the plans and hands of the wicked and ungodly.

4. That you would surrender yourself and all that concerns you to the Lord.

5. That you would realize tests come as opportunities for growth and development.

6. You would understand that your perception of events in your life will determine your outcome.

7. My prayer for you is that your prayer life would develop—pray without ceasing, about everything.

8. Finally, that you remember what God says about you and know that he is ever-present with you.

Examples of defining moments

From God or the enemy?

- "If you didn't have a heart for the Lord, I wouldn't waste my time dating you."

- "You'll never amount to anything!"

- "You looked good when you were skinny," this was said to a full-figured lady.

- "You're just like your daddy," coming from the mouth of a broken, neglected woman, she said to her daughter.

- "Girl, you got it going on and don't even know it," speaking of my ministry and the love I have for the Lord.

- "I am ugly," this is from a woman who had been told that as a little girl by her family.

- "Mama's baby, daddy's maybe," words spoken from the mouth of the man that the baby was conceived with.

- Went in for eye repair surgery and came out with the eye worse than before.

- "I bet not catch you wearing makeup because you don't need it!"

- "You evil black witch," yelled because a person did not feel like talking about a soap opera that both were sitting there watching at the same time.

- "You can't come to my church because you won't agree with my teaching on women!"

- "You should not be teaching on the retreat because your husband is not walking right," in response, the woman had to be made aware that I had a true relationship with Father God before I got married.

- Someone says to their son, "I only married your mother because she was thick," the young man's mother is much smaller than years ago.

- "Every man wants a ghetto woman," needless to say that was the last day I saw that man because he found a ghetto woman with no love for herself and care for what God did on the cross to break us free from the bondage of sin over us.

- A pregnant woman was told by the father of her baby, "Don't ask me to do anything for you because I did not want another child," the woman was on bedrest and doing all she could to hold this child in her womb.

- "Hey, I didn't know you were pretty, I knew your sisters were pretty, but I didn't know you were!"

- "I knew you were going to be sick in life because you did not take the medication I told you to take."

- "You need to be like your sister!"

- "Can you still have children? I wouldn't mind having a little girl, just like you!"

- "I can't put you on a pedestal, because you don't share your secret areas with me."

- Pregnant and spotting, but left with no help or concern for me or the baby's outcome—remember God is always there with you.

- "You didn't know how to be a wife, you didn't have any good examples of marriage!"

- Visiting a patient in a memorial medical center in long beach, which was my dad, and I was laying my hand on my dad's chest, praying for his healing because he was having a hard time breathing and a voice calls out to me, "Get your hand off my dad's chest" this was from my sister that I thought knew who I really was in Christ Jesus, and the power that we know is allowed in the laying on of hands for the sick in the name of Jesus.

- "I can accomplish many things with you by my side!"

- "I wanted your voice to be the last one I heard before I faced my challenging, unknown day!"

- I have one for the books for you—how about having a close friend of yours set you up. There was a woman who had a great friend that she always spoke highly of, even to her boyfriend, her boyfriend decided that he wanted to pursue the woman she spoke so highly of to see if the woman was what his girl said she was. This poor in spirit, low in standard wounded girl watched as her boyfriend pursued a relationship with another woman right in front of her face. The girl did and said nothing to stop it. She could've thrown a monkey wrench in the whole thing before any other relationship could've developed, but she kept her mouth closed walking around angry and lying to her friends. Instead of handling it like a woman, she played games on the phone, having another woman, her neighbor, call the lady trying to scare her. The scary thing is, that this girl made some serious threats, she said, "I started to kill him, first, I started to have my sons beat him up," all because he turned his interest from her. This person also turned out to be a stalker, a stalker of the lady and of the man she knew when and where each one had been at various times. God is a God of forgiveness! "Father forgive them for they know not what they've done!"

REFLECTIONS

Your prayer life should definitely increase now, if not for you, then for all that may be going through defining times in their lives.

If your mind surmised a hurtful outcome to those who dealt with any of those defining moments, pray that the Lord would heal them and make them whole.

*I pray that in the forefront of your mind is the very thought that the Lord is always with us!

Matthew 7:12 (NIV), says, "So in everything, do to others what you would have them do to you, for this sums up the Law and the Prophets."

There are many situations in life that can impact you, leaving you; crippled, baffled, wounded, scared, and broken, but God! Do not let trying times define you, stand on the word of God, and allow God to fight your battles for you, so you will remain a vessel of honor and a conduit of love.

Our perspective of what we are dealing with and why we are dealing with it, will determine our outcome in trying times.

Tests in life are opportunities for growth and development in the lives of God's children.

One's true character is shown during testing times. Is your integrity and character developed enough to resist the devil and to stand as a vessel of honor unto the Lord and surrender unto God with a yes in the tempting times?

BEAUTY

Gorgeous are you girl,
Your beauty, is none like.
From the sway of your hips,
To the pose you strike!
An inner beauty, you expel,
From the flow of your wise words,
To the echoes of your encouragement,
And the hearts, you up gird!
Your beauty excels all,
As God intended it to be,
No secret to the world,
For the Lord made you, you see!
Precious in every way,
From your inside to your out,
Rooted and grounded in the word
Awesomely formed, no doubt!
Your struggles have been many;
You've overcome every one,
Making you God's chosen.
For his greater work to be done
—By Shirley D.

SPEAK!

If names you want to hurl,
Try this on for size,
Jesus, Jesus, Jesus,
Oh so, awesome and wise!
Words can be powerful,
Bringing forth life or death,
Choose your words wisely,
As to not waste your breath!
Every moment is precious,
For God gives us life,
Make sure not to waste it,
Unaware of your eternal flight.
Every breath we breathe,
To the moves we make,
Are orchestrated in God's plan,
Getting us ready, for heaven's sake!
Whether you name it,
Believe, or claim it,
Jesus is;
And to him, we must submit!
Speak!
—By Shirley D.

MIRROR

Questioning what I look like,
With curiosity and delight,
I'm lead to find out,
Although with apprehension and fright!
Finally making it to the mirror,
Beholding my face in a glass,
Vision of me becomes clearer,
Focusing my eyes at last.
In my ears I hear,
"Oh my child, what do you see?"
I answered I see you Lord,
Through your word looking at me.
Gazing in the mirror,
Wondering how I fare,
Examining my walk with you Lord,
As to your word how I compare!
—By Shirley D.

BIBLIOGRAPHY

Ryrie, Caldwell, Charles THD, PhD
The Ryrie Study Bible—English Standard Version (ESV)
2007 Publication
Chicago
Moody Publishers
Acts 17:28, Esther chapter 1, Isaiah chapter 46, Psalm 139:1–5, 13–16, Leviticus 19:18, St. John 10:10, Hebrews 13:5, Psalm 4:13
The Hebrew Greek Key Study Bible
King James Version revised edition 1991
United States of America
AMG Publishers, AMG International Inc.
Matthew 28:19, Romans 8:28, 1 Thessalonians 5:16, James 1:17, Philippians 4:19, Ephesians 2:10, 4:14, St. John 3:16, Proverbs 3:5–6, Psalm 24:1, the book of Daniel, 2 Corinthians 2:14
Life Application Study Bible
New Living Translation Red Letter Edition
Second edition October 2007
Carol steam Illinois
Tyndale House Publishers Inc.
Romans 8:27, Ephesians 1:4
The New York International Bible Society

The Holy Bible

New International Version copyright 1978

Grand Rapids, Michigan

Zondervan Bible Publishers

Ephesians 6:10–18, Isaiah 45:22, 1 Corinthians 9:24–27, Hebrews 12:1–2, 1 Peter 2:9, Romans 5:8, Philippians 4:7–8, Job 32:6–8, St. Luke 12:7, Jeremiah 29:11–13, Judges 16, Deuteronomy 31:6, Matthew 22:39, 2 Peter 3:1

Life Application Bible

New King James Version (NKJV)

1993

Wheaton, Illinois

Tyndale House Publishers Inc.

Psalm 139:13–14, 1 Samuel 1:10–17, Philippians 4:6, Psalm 37:5

Google search engine

Larry Page and Sergey Brin

September 4, 1998

You Tube

Chad Hurley, Steve Chen, Jawed Karim

February 14, 2005

Subsidiary of Google

Helen Baylor, "Wounded Soldier, Minister Mervin Mayo: He knows my name," and "What kind of man," Donald Lawrence and the Tri-City Singers, "I am God" and Jason Nelson, "Forever."

Donald Lawrence Tri-City Singers

Album finale act one, "I am God"# 13

April 4, 2006

Jason Nelson

Album- "The answer – song forever" #5

Jason Nelson

May 18, 2018
Helen Baylor
Album –highly recommended– "Wounded Soldier" #9
Word Entertainment
1990

ACKNOWLEDGMENTS

In everything, give thanks, for this is the will of God in Christ Jesus concerning you (1 Thess. 5:18, KJV). It is a blessing and an honor to be at this place in my life, being able to share part of my life with all who will read this book. To God be the glory for all he has done, in and through me, as a testament to his faithfulness, love, and power.

I am so thankful for those in life who pushed me through adversity to learn of my worth. It seems so weird, but I thank the Lord, now, for the abusive, inconsiderate people I've encountered in my journey of finding out who Shirley is. Bullies in my younger days influenced me to do better and to treat others with love and compassion. Being able to acknowledge negative folks and the impact they had on developing me into who I am is something I want to give thanks for.

Heartfelt thanks goes out to my family who supported me in my endeavors in life, and even those who laughed at me when I shared things I was working toward. I must give thanks to my son, Zaire, my personal encourager, and sounding board to some of my writings. It is a blessing for me to say thanks to the Harts,

Hales, Hunters, Conleys, Mills, Adkinsons, and the Livingstons for helping me realize that I am loved, and purposed in life.

In acknowledging special folks in my life, I must give shout-outs to the Friday night Christian young people fellowship, who encouraged me to boldly use the gifts the Lord had given me, even confidently allowing me to minister. Great thanks and appreciation to the New Hope Baptist Church of Long Beach for my Christian upbringing, and to the New Horizon MBC of Lynwood; Ralph Turner Jr., Pastor along with the Women of Grace Ministry in the same church. Thanks to Greater Big Bethel, of Watts, under the leadership of Pastor Mark Carroll, Greater Cornerstone of Los Angeles, One Lord One Faith One Baptism of North Long Beach, Hope of Glory of Compton, Christ Christian Home of Compton, COA Ministry of Long Beach, and Calvary Baptist Church of Compton, all being instrumental in speaking life into me and aiding me in maturing in my mental, spiritual, and physical areas of life

Last but not least, to my godchildren: DeAndre, Marlin, Jasmine, and Andrew; to my godbrothers Andre and Dwight, all my extended family, my prayer partner, Henrietta Johnson, every last one of my nieces and nephews, my adopted family, my brother and my two sons who are in the presence of the Lord, I must give special recognition for the impact each of you had on my life. God bless each of you for being a blessing to me!

Know the Author

Shirley Hart, born in Torrance, California, to Coleman and Judith Hart, descendants of greatness. I am one of four children born to this union. As a family-oriented person, I champion the cause of fighting for family unity, anyone's family.

Loving the Lord as a young child graced me to love him even into adulthood, causing me to desire to share that love with all I can. I am a person that uses all that God has gifted me with to bring joy to others. God has blessed me with craft creativity: T-shirt designing skills, greeting card creations, obituary writing techniques, making bereavement and homeless love care packages, and writing poems of comfort, teaching Sunday schools, mission classes, conference meetings, and teaching in public and private schools opened up an opportunity for me to bring joy to more people.

Writing poetry, reading my poetry at various venues, and entering poetry contests on rhyme zone and poetry. Com has brought me great joy as I was able to share Jesus with a wider audience. One of my poems, "Gone Away" was published in poetry. com's collected whispers 2008 edition. Teaching, publicly speaking, and writing for years, I've now decided to share my writings on a greater public scale.

Being blessed by the giver of life to birth three sons, though two of them are in his presence, I am eternally grateful for my MVP, Zaire, who I can share my passions for: life, love, ministry, and writing with. I consider myself a champion to bring change, for the better. I fight for the mistreated, the jailed, and those who seek for a second chance at a better life. As I educate myself, I also seek to educate others, and as I grow in knowledge, I open the door for others to grow as well.

I have a heart for ministry to minister to the hurt, wounded, disgusted, broken, discouraged, abused, confused, unsheltered, sinful people, and all who desire to know the true love of God. Experiencing each one of those areas in my own life has allowed me to become sensitive to others who have undergone the same treatment causing me to develop a passion to help them become whole.